Snow grotesque? What's exaggerated here contra the o.g. Wonder Tale or Disney's dewy take where the sopped and swollen melisma was a three-explosion euphemism of gimme gimme? To amplify's not to over-blow; Lara Glenum cranks up the horny anxiety of a Kween's "Who's the fairest of them all" and duels it against a princess who knows her prince will cum. Knives out. What *SNOW* slashes hardest even as its protagonists lacerate-to-limn daughter/mother tropes is the fairy tale that a woman's desire mitigates her exploitation or assault. And Glenum does this brutal bladework with ferocity, leaving every body fluid on the castle's floors but tears. This isn't Snow White updated and subverted; nope, it's Snow White stripped back to wet bone and seeping eros, to bloody appetite and junk power, to sublime dirt and dirt and dirt. —**DOUGLAS KEARNEY**

One of our greatest living poets, Lara Glenum's sorcery on the page is unmatched. Her work is bawdy, ingenuous, glittering. *SNOW* is Glenum at the pinnacle of her powers. Through this darkest of fairy tales, Glenum holds up the Evil Kween's occult mirror, revealing our archaic nightmares alongside our latest, trickiest "punishment cupboards." "A princess is a junk meme & I'm a junk means by which power asserts" *SNOW* proclaims, for at its splayed-on-a-platter heart, this is a story of a mother and a daughter pitted against one another by techno-necro-patriarchal-capitalism. Horny and violent and oozing and candy and strange, *SNOW* is a singular work of art. —**KATE DURBIN**

SNOW

Lara Glenum

Action Books   Notre Dame, IN   2024

Action Books

Joyelle McSweeney and Johannes Göransson, Founding Editors
Katherine Hedeen and Paul Cunningham, Managing Editors
Camille Lendor and Noah Loveless, Editorial Assistants 2023–2024
Shanna Compton, Book Design

First Edition

ISBN: 978-0-900575-19-8
Library of Congress Control Number: 2023951129

Cover art: Camille Rose Garcia, *Leaky Refuge* (2011).

For more information, please contact us at
Action Books, 233 Decio Hall, Notre Dame, IN 46556

or visit
actionbooks.org

"What is the communal vision of poetry if you are
curved, odd, indefinite, irregular, feminine."
—Susan Howe

"Mirrors are the doors through which death comes and goes."
—Jean Cocteau, *Orfée*

THE HUNT'S AFOOT

THE POISON LODGE

THIS DEATH DROP
IS FOR ALL YOU MIRACLES
ICED BY THE WICKEDS

LET IT SNOW

LET IT SNOW

A witch baby

I blubber out
into empire's hooks

I warble out
a curl-i-cue girlsong

Swipe left to abort
my future
Swipe right

& Kerpow
I level up

to a darkbright
mutinous new world

DEAR PRINCE HARMING

I'm unbossed & sinking

in the guts of the hour
I'm corrupt in the guts

of your gluey warbling
I'm strung out like blow

in a bubbling sky
You're a smart boy

You don't believe
this nonsense

You go south & starkers
& various other kewl appointments

I don't care

With my vixen soul whip
& my max glands rising

I bite hard   until you let go
& My spirit animal's
disemboweled

& served up
in pink meringue floats

Too easily words of war
Become acts of war

It's time we reviewed
the accounts

You need to know just how much
this is going to cost you

THE ACID KWEEN

At meat o'clock
I expire
My skin drags magnetic south
My heart ulcers

are full of poodles
My scabbed scalp

is a screamer
The whack of ages

& I'm being chummed
into a meat cloud
Stank oceans roil

Hell
is a ripe daughter

ALLOWANCE

Mommy Mommy
Can I have a gun

to shoot down the butchers
of childhood

I need my own cash
to buy splooge grenades

& lethal fireworks
for rape holidays

Mommy
Why do you keep paying me
bullets to the skull

MIRROR!
MIRROR!

MIRROR MIRROR

Like you
I'm a royal eyebeast
A gaper   at miseries
         I double down
A scrying glass
     I'll pop
       that lazy eye
& crack up
your pity party
     Stop
this legendary bitch-brawl
with your mother
Snowflake
       Speak to me
       O Poster Girl for fragility
       at its loudest
& Most lethal
weapons explode in the hands
of the maker
       Are you the bomb
Or the maker
Speak to me O Suicide
bomber laced into dynamite
tulle vestware

Make a move
Miss White
& It'll damn sure kill you

DAUGHTER CELLS / DAUGHTER SELLS

Can you sever the painloop
                playing out across the centuries
Mothers slicing into daughters

Daughters biodegrading at the speed of light

A daughter is a crime scene
A ready-made
      murder victim   Gleaming like a singing cutlet
                        Hogtied
                        to the crackling family hearth
      Wild-eyed rodent starlet
      electrocuted by her own squealing demons
Neck-broke
Teeth popping out like popcorn

The juiciest role
The least well paid

Except for the mother   who can be played by any ghastly
      old roadkill
Any burbling old meatlump   wielding a milktit & a cleaver

THE FAIREST OF THEM ALL

SNOW
Mother is bleeding up new crime scenes
Her poisonfingers drawing lethal rings around snapping necks
     Mother is toxic lethal contagious
        & I'm a corrupt copy
of her ambivalent love

MAGYK MIRROR
Stop your goo goo wailing
in that janky box
All's not lost
Mimesis is magic
The oldest occult technology
The Illusion of the Real
      Let's make a deal
          You show me
          & I'll show you
    Reflect on this Snowflake
I can be of use

SNOW
Shut your piehole Mirror

MAGYK MIRROR

O well said Teen Kween
Did they teach you that
in art skool

                Catch up Hotcakes
      In this story
I am the portal through which Death comes and goes
You want in
You want out
      You go through me

SNOW

Skedaddle phantom
I've yanked all the lights out of me
Pigswill sloshing in a dim box
I reflect nothing

MAGYK MIRROR

Your mother lies deathly ill
      Her luxe wig askew
      Her iron teeth clang
The candy-cane windows of her eyes melted out
& Still
she calls for you in achebright tones

COME HOME COME HOME
MY DARLING GIRL

SNOW
Christ
What do you even want

MAGYK MIRROR
As long as you live & breathe
in that buttery skin
I want what's mine
Which is to say

I want what's yours

You think you can defuse
        this royal clusterfuck
by playing dead
You can't abdicate
so easily
Baby girl
        You can wear the crown
or burn it down
Kaboom

SNOW
Wait
Who's even speaking

Mom is that—

THE ONLY SAFE PLACE
IS
UNDER MY SKIRTS

PALACE
DAYS

MOTHER'S LITTLE HELPER

I'm a doozie
of a wild witch
     Kween of the Undermundo   I fake out deathstars
        with my magyk mirror
Heads roll & pump
sex grease
     in tribute to my booty

So I drink the blood of virgins
So what
Who doesn't
      That's patriarchy for you   Who am I
   to claim I'm on the outside
        So I'm a bottom-feeder So the heck what
Bottom's up!
can only mean one thing
      when there's a boot on your neck

DADHOLE

Mommy & I are haggling
About ancestry

She says witches
I say vampires
She only punches me

because I'm evil

I sucknuzzle Mommy
into a pile of smiling milk

AFTER SCHOOL SPECIAL / LEGAL DEPENDENT

Mommy is a laughing crypto
cannibal   Her long saber teeth
enclose my face
People mistake it for a crown
Still
I keep a steady head
        I'm smiling & chirruping
I'm beaming
my girlstar I make Mommy proud Until I accidentally break
her entire life
        & She retracts her sabers & then
I'm a cartoon fountain
spurting
real blood   in this cracked-up marble courtyard

My head falls off

PAINT THE TOWN RED

Snowflake
keeps vandalizing our city walls
with the hair of all those disappeared girls
dipped in red paint

Protest art lmao

It's so tragic
How did
she even find the graves
where I buried them

CANCEL CULTURE

Mirror Mirror
My diamond cloak of nerves
got downvoted
        & Now I'm in the punishment cupboard
spitting up the tiny bones of children

Mirror Mirror
What's a girl to do
     Late stage capitalism's at the murder-helm
I'm reduced
to peddling relics & fifty-cent hand jobs

        All those glandular mirages
& lubricated lightning bolts
can't help me now   My brain's like an alien bouquet
pulsating above me
on the ceiling

SORRY I RUINED YOUR LIFE

Today Mommy is wigging out in a towering headpiece
Mommy spams me with hate mail & I'm at the mercy
   of her criminal administration

of howlers
This colossal wreck

is all my fault
I broke the bank
    I need to pay for her persecution mania
  & royal boxes
of skittery chompers

so she can finally fix

Her demolished body
Her sky-ripping tears

PARENTING IS TRASH

We are all the child of something stank
& murderous Dumpling
Even the brightest homes eat death
on the down-low

Why my own mom

CHILDREN SHOULD BE KILLED NOT HEARD

At the dinner table
you demand 500 years

of silence
And hand me my clit

on a plate

pierced by a tiny flag

emblazoned with
the ensign of our house
A rotting sun

whose zany beams
tickle my eyes into stones
& burn out

my vocal cords
The open cavity in my throat

is a shrine
to our new & improved day

HOME SICK

Snowflake's got
a blotto case
     of garbage body
          Patient zero gtfo

How dare you
get the plague
You monstrous doe-eyed cliché
    Get up
You're not sick lollipop girl
            Goddamn apex predator
            in disguise
    A glass coffin
Really?
You wanna play?   It's your funeral
          The diseased have no rights
After all
I'm the one who shot you
    out of my shunt
    I'll sure as hell shoot you again

GIRL DO YOUR HOMEWORK

Snowflake
is holed up   in her bratlab again
          conjuring wet pain   through a magyk screen
Chatting up
Prince Harming
          That dopey scion of the Royal House of Ugh
                  An illustrious male line   of hot spooks
who made their kazillions
                          from data mining & black-ops
          Revenge porn &
bad performance art   Haters
                              to the core

MILKHEX

Mommy's mewling milk
is chock with hexes

& shiny shards
I yank down into

my cryptoself
Wailing in the mirror room

I sprain the faces
of my demon lovers
A wrecking ball

is a girl whose pain
has been outsourced

to trolls &
stupid dwarves

SHUT THE FREAKING DOOR

In my skank wig
            I'm drilling down
        into the sexosphere   Looking for
                                    Prince Harming

& his mad rad cancerous
flunked-out joy

I send an emoji to the Prince
            hiding out in the No Zone
        with his rebel legions

An hour later   I'm snorting discount hexes
& cutting off all my hair
       when his voice bounces in on hot gold springs
lubing up the terror portal
       on my amazing
       phantom third channel

SLEEPER CELLS AWAKE

I'm overthrowing my house
he says

Boy Bye
I say
I'm busy

trying to stay alive
The points of his teeth
gleam high

He laughs & says
I can blow up big
like him

& take my entire house
with me
I can show you how it's done
He grins
& slides his fingers
into the wet velvet lining
      of my coffin

MIDWINTER
BALL

I DON'T NEED NO KINGIE

Howl now
Mirror
                It's party time
        Help me
shed this cracked-ass carcass

        I'm gonna pile all those boys
into my bedazzled maw
Dangle them dripping wet

over all me holes &
        horn out   into the fried lime greens of spring
on me half-starved
wolf legs

COSPLAY GONE WRONG

Pop my cherry
I'm a royal

criminal I swallow
a blood blister

pod on the tree of
Ding Dong

& Dang This boy's dead
& I still don't feel

a thing
Clean up this bloody mess

Snowflake
& Feed me my crown

in reverse
Fade out this junky fatal accident

This weeping kingdom
of useless cum

PUNK DEBUTANTE

In a gilded ballroom
The wrecking ball flies

into my mouth
And I suck it

down until I cataclysm
Until I pop and lock
I'm ok I'm loaded

with weeping insects
I can live without medics

or even a home
I'm just a weeping animal

in dire need of a disco bullet
to my singing skullmeat

DANCE CARD

Please excuse me
if I pass
on your very kind offer Sir
            but I'm about to explode
under my own sinewy spell
        in this too-tight baller gown

Excuse me if I pass Kind Sir
I'm really
only interested
in coming hard

& not with you

Why is female pleasure such a threat
Darling
You're really a very dull beast
An insult to leaping animals

A travesty to skipping girls

MIDWINTER BALLING

The wigwalkers purl in every corridor
                    Golden horrors popping in their knickers
        & I'm skeered
        like a glamoured rat
     My thumper goes all twitchy

       I'm young   I'm a cheap raiding party
        The wigwalkers   try to lick me through my panties
     while I order sow hearts online
& torch them   to achieve hologram-perfect skin

       I float through the afterparty in a mist of blood
       to hide
       my perfect febrile knobs
               I so badly need to get twisted
before I gag on my own black bile
     It Girl Shit Girl

I'm a photo filter called Rot
At the venom burst
At the shooting   I make snow angels
in dumpfields of red sewage
          Even the decaying musculature
     of snowflakes
looks good on me

The black lace of fried nerves
I eat off my own legs
like a delicacy

MIDNIGHT ARRIVAL

Prince Harming dismounts
The sky bows low
The animals stomp & grind

The grass grows wet
supine under his winking boot

No one can stop staring
at his crotch

WHAT A CREAMY JOLT IN THE FANCYPANTS

O my
Look at Prince Harming
My how that boy's grown

I'm cuntstruck
by the luscious buck

I take my cream hard
I like my young bloods stiff
with deathswoon
But the prince

who just rolled up
is an annihilation
I'm eye-fucking
a marvel of a bucking

young Prince
at the height of
his clit-shaking powers

KISS MY ROYAL HAND

Pop open
those cosmic eyes Princeling   Blink once for Yes
      Twice for YAASSSSSS

you will be my slippery astral bitch
        Come out firing
on all cocks & climb onto my vixen slag heap
Yes Lawd Rang-a-lang You can come You can go

deaf from all the pleasure My pleasure valves
go pop
Same as any goddamn gun

THE ROYAL HOUSE OF UGH

The laughing prince
is an erotic
weather cell

The court is in upheaval
Swoons & fits over his brocade pants
splitting
in a heavenly river of agitprop   His steamy
baroque swagger

Our bones
are crawling out of our poor bodies
& ooching across the floor
just trying to reach him

I LEFT MY ♥ ON THE DANCE FLOOR

This party is decaying
into a pleasuredome
on a celestial scale

    In the mosh pit
    angels lube up & sing
    Burn down the state

The prince grabs my hand
Our mutual extinction
incandesces & pops

& in a high-yield organ system
we pivot & twist
    Miracles zinging
off our skins
like slaughter

Twilight clangs
I can hear the stars chewing

Nearby
bombs start falling

EXPLOSION 1

A holy volley
of lightning
sings off

the darling body
of the Prince

Like a strike
to the throat-vault
my lungs are tied off

This hyperbeauty
in gold-braided raiment

of exploding suns
rolls dice
carved from my wailing

jumping bones
& EVERY single time
he rolls those
maddening hips

I win

EXPLOSION 2

I'm going to bleed out now
I don't care if it's fatal

candy
It's weeping in my mouth
His colossal

sweetness makes me so horny
I could puke

up my entire future
In a burst
of sex magyk I'm coming a jubilee of

Hot Damn
Baby's gotta have it
Get me down

on my knees
& I rule the world

EXPLOSION 3

Stick your stiff deity into my spunkbox
& I'll gift you

The Hanged Man
My meatfrills turbo-swell

Fucking Christ
I'm going to come

right out of my girlsockets
It's glorious out here

where the world licks & dips
& ends

DIRTY ARTS

You psychotic fetus

The palace is collapsing
& here you are   smearing the bright world
                with your shit
I hope you drown
in your own cuntbutter

Everything you love
buckles & warps

I THINK YOU MISTOOK ME FOR AN ASSWIPE

or a feebleminded
toad-hole
to hide your murder junket

A+ Good job
for all your
secret failures
        Gold stars raining down on us
like phosphorescent lions of all your imperial wars
Like stank spoils   of perma-toxic ruin

Bring on your reign
of weeping junk
All your
kingdoms   are now blowing up
                with shit

GIRLBOMB

In black bombazine
I turbogut
your killing voice   I scuttle our doomy future

I go off in public on repeat repeat Blow
I'm a junk siren
going off
          my own alarm-rigged skin
This foul house

I waste now & now
A spectacle unloading   across suffering kingdoms
A princess
is a junk meme & I'm a junk means
              by which power asserts
       What & Who
-ever are you I advise you to run
My body is interrupted
with killing light

Don't try this at home kids
Don't look at the deadly motherlight
Self-immolation is for garbage gamines like me
A case of the wickeds
          will surely kill you

SO THIS IS HOW YOU REPAY ME

Don't think
    for a hot sec   you'll get off
    without paying dearly for all the shit you pull
    $$$$$
You'll do tricks for me
Snowflake   Even in the grave

I'll hunt you down the centuries
I'll burn the heart   right out of you
    You little shit   I slay
You pay
me bank   Not those idiot   floppy smiles
full
    of girlsick

THE HUNT'S
AFOOT

BRING ME HER HEART ON A PLATTER

That counterfeit
screwball waif is not my daughter
She's some rando who's after my cashbox

    "Out to kill her" wtf
How absurd
Why I've been a champion of the grubby snotty & grotty
    for years

I ask you
Who's the real threat to the state here
I ask you
Who needs to be skinned alive

INTO THE WOODS

The Royal Hunter's a royal cunt
who services the Kween

A berserker   A grotty lurker   with a mil kills
& a whopper piece
                 .for popping scofflaws

              In the Lightning Reeks
         He's hard on
              my tail   He does "The Hunter's Boogaloo"
firing creamy bullets
              into my dumpskins
The goop of
miracles & then the ax falls

on my smoking hams
& He's balls deep   in the piglight
& We do
the wild animal switcheroo   Mommy
                           can't tell my swineheart
                 from a pig's

A TASTE OF VICTORY

Nom Nom   Her swiney thumper
on a platter
tickles my brittle flank

My rank veins flash freak sugars
My skin pinks   My clit perks

How now Magyk Mirror

IF I ONLY HAD A COMPASS

This forest ain't no party
Angel Britches

So many creepers
& broke-neck witches
swinging in trees   Ghastly showgirls

I go feral &
the sky goes bloop

but I can't see it
Small animals

keep dry-humping
my leg

STAY SHINY

My stanky eyes crumple

all over Boom Boom Mountain
Where garbage boys trill

& drill in marshmallow firebursts
I toss a wolf head

into their gang magyk
I drive my tasteless death-rig

all over their futile posse
Ghosts spew blood-curlicues
I accidentally fall asleep

in the murder museum
& Some stupid monster appears
All dangly tubes & drippy blubber
& I can't stop

dreaming about you
My valentine lobes grow long &
I knock you

into my swinging contagion
I accidentally try to explode your heart
I accidentally block your arteries

with my flaming car
I gum up your crimesoaked eye

My accidental lifestyle
among loons
is now for sale

NEGGING

Tick tock
I pop & lock

at the end of my rope
Hellfreak
Suicide
Gallows bride
O look

Here come
the Chuckle Scouts

Seven squealing miners
They're practically soiling
their codpieces

What a wild mercy
They cut me down

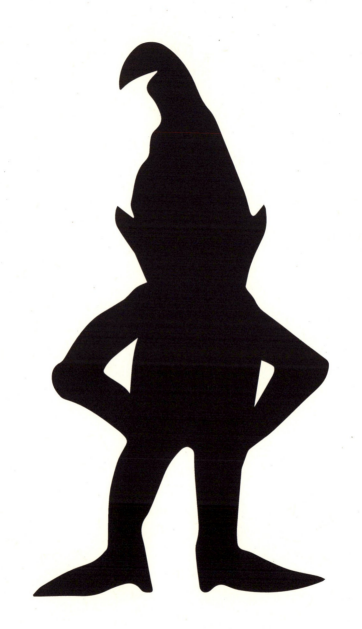

BIOHACKERS

They call us
    Wealth-suckers of the Storm Sun
    Guardians of the Bone Marsh
    Extraction Kings of the Solar Hole

We're but humble data miners
(butt-humble
ha!)
Practical machines for any wayward ingenue
We bag & boost
We data dredge
    Spike neural networks at bargain rates

Yes ma'am
We're humble miners
Not a men's rights group or black-ops cyber-militia
        Not flunkies of the crown
But Snow White
(the skank)
keeps calling us trolls

CLUSTER ANALYTICS

It's terrible math
The tiny men multiply
  & now they're scraping dinner
out of knickers I left on the floor

I dig around in a tin can & find a wiry tail
  I try it on
  It fits like a dream

of my own cute buttery extinction
Of high-speed
human trafficking

REVENGE PORN

The data miners
   are up to their giggle
         in bitecoin
The latest occult technology   They siphon out souls
      & project them nude onto cloudglobs
Seekers roll their eyes

through bone-loops
& butt swag

Vision's the bomb
Just by looking
      you can blow
      so many girls to crying pieces

DWARFSTAR MURDER PARTY

Seven bright hells
decorate my starblown face
          You force-feed me your idiocy
                    Swellhearts
& It smells like gala cum
Down in the blitz

the data mines are opening
& I'm sweeping out
              this dwarf fantasy
          You high-maintenance bitches

like to string me from the chandelier
                    Apple in my mouth
                              I do the dirty
                              I do the entire room
          I suck out all that poison
          with my charmed headgear
I suck
until I shine like rising death
          I shine until   I'm rotten rotten
                              to the core

THE
POISON
LODGE

DEAR DEAD KING

I was the Abominable Bride
& you were
an icon of the miraculous

One of us had to go

But I only wanted to give you
a light maiming
& some mouth opera

when you came tilting at me
with your crimson biggie

On the Horn of the Moon
I'm breaking dawn's pink fingers
one by one

Your axeblades
still stuck in my back
like wings

I fly out over
our still-smoldering swamp

YOO
HOO

WHERE
ARE
YOU

TRICKSY BEGGAR LADY

Knock Knock
Snowflake

Let a poor old woman in

I'm shivering in me lardy bits
in this assweather

Give us some shelter
won't you
& a little brawling hot punch

MOMMY'S AT THE DOOR WAGGLING HER BRIGHT BONE

Where is your Mother
Princess
Why you're totally falling apart

For God's sake
lace up your whalebone corset
before you sag to death

At least let me
        get you your meds
Why I've got them right here

I've seen your outlaw Prince
That's one delicious piece
of hellmeat

I'll sell you

A comb to fix your hairball
A jewel
for your sad boondoggled muff

AN APPLE A DAY

The only exit
is though the wormhole

in the apple
I bite into you

so I can vanish
Mommy made a bad thing
in my laces

& now I'm snaking out
on the floor
I'm foaming &

It's bad fits
Like a virgin

abortion I plop
& drop

HARD CORE

Your exploding heart
is not my problem

I worm into your acehole
& poke around
for a creamy victory

You're gonna get licked
Every valve & crevice

is gonna blow

CHOKECHERRY

In the poison lodge
My spine
begins fusing together   I see animals strung up
in trees   In psychomotor groves
Grief
is blowing through me on tornadic legs
I lose all my eyes
        I'm spilling across a thousand floors

The world is ending
& still you keep

hunting me down the brightbursting eons
in the brittle mask

of a mother

I open my voice
like the ripped-open stomach
of a sacrificial animal
Oracular & bloody

This is a kind of singing

A red spasm of light
in never-ending dark

My eyes go black from end to end & reverb
in a blind pooling
Black ripples to the edges of me

Stars crawl into my joints & explode
My hands twitch with spiders of light

The floating world
chokes & exhales

The state is full of murder holes like me

Girls with burst red faces
In a chapel of bone   I thread a needle
through our eye
Ham flowers bloom among burial mounds
Spectral echoes of flesh vining up

THIS SHOW HAS BEEN CANCELED

I'm not going to make it out alive
Or to some fabled
other side

There is no other side

to this tale
Only the pitch

& buckle of a mind
too long overstrained

My past keeps
dragging me back

When I try to wade
to the other side

of the stream
the far shore keeps vanishing

My perceptual errors
are endless

GOODBYE

Mommy is dropping acid
all over my life
Super-saturate acid spitholes lobslobbering down skinwalls opening
Doors
In the palace outhouse   I'm tricked out in private
Inside-out twists of my acid-soaked mind high high high hi

hi haints
Greetings guests popping out of every grate
Greetings to
this ghoulish howl-drama bright like infanticide

Greetings to the child you blasted
with phantasmagoria The child was crying
over a bleeding dog

Now I come at the wrong times
in all the wrong places
with all the wrong people levitating via my body

Where is the agency

Which agency do I apply to
To stop the trains running

My mother is running trains

I am still small
I'm crying over my bleeding dog
    You scoff & go slobbering into the gunroom
    where you sleep in acidgold foil
Mother
You close the door

Every night I wake
I hear you approaching The swish of your skirts as you castle over me
I fever
I'm shaking & retching I crawl to the door It won't open
The ghost children are biting me

      Bites welting up all over my hips & thighs
I have to stay silent
If I wish to stay alive

My mother is running trains

What does the train look like
Well I'm blindfolded I can't see anything But I hear the men come in
one after another
Men of state pomp & rigged circumstances
of power   I'm forever in their favor
        A party favor bleeding into their shoes & hair
When they get off me   which is never

I'm hemorrhaging clots out
This is the blot-out

I exist as a blister of pleasure
I am treason
set against the state
I need rapture not rapeture
I open my aperture
& seize I seize I'm seized I seize
up

My mother keeps running trains
She's queen
      & This virgin nation must crackle & reverb
with seismic splendor
This country must be efficient Must made to be run on time
& The economy is booming all over my chest The empire is rising
& slamming into halls of justice where
                        harm is seed in my childhair

My body's a dread clock
My sprawling legs strike the hour & regulate power Never mine
Never mine
Never mind
The office of propaganda says *This is Victory*

Remember our history
says the Kween   looking over timetables again distracted
& handing me a wipe

ACKNOWLEDGMENTS

I owe a huge debt of gratitude to Johannes Göransson and the editorial team at Action Books for bringing this book to fruition. I'm very grateful to Chris Rovee, who gave me shelter and space, and to Kate Durbin, who got me through. This book would also not have been possible without the sharp editorial eye of Elizabeth Kolenda. Thanks to the Vermont Studio Center and to LSU for giving me material support during the completion of this project. Inexpressible thanks to my beloved family, particularly my mom for her unflappable faith in me, and my two rapscallions for filling my days with so much joy.

Thanks to the editors of *Fence*, *Fanzine*, *Tarpaulin Sky*, and *Burning House Press*, in which poems from this book appeared.

ABOUT THE AUTHOR

Lara Glenum is the author of four books of poetry, including *Pop Corpse*, *Maximum Gaga*, *The Hounds of No*, and *All Hopped Up On Fleshy Dumdums*, a limited edition art book. Her poetry has been described as "a splattered fairy tale for today, a new flavor of poetic candy, and, ultimately, a pleasure to read." She teaches literature and creative writing at LSU.